Kids and Family History

History

Fun Ways to Spark Their Interest

I0437225

Vicki Korn Niggemeyer

DENVER, COLORADO

Dedicated to my wonderful children and grandchildren

who will one day be the keepers of our family histories!

Jeffrey – John – Jennifer

Tori - JD – Connor – Jocelyn - Cooper

Also by Vicki Korn Niggemeyer

Holydays Holidays (co-authored with Judith Ritchie)

Get Creative with Your Family History

Contents

1

It's Never Too Soon to Start!

It is a well-known fact that young children learn quickly. We teach them to count. We teach them colors. We teach them the alphabet. Soon they master those then are well on their way to reading and doing simple math. So why should family history be any different?

Our kids and grandkids easily learn who mommy and daddy are. As well as grandpa and grandma. So, there you go, the very beginnings of a family tree. And it was so simple! Adding great-grandparents, aunts and uncles, cousins and more is indeed another layer; but children sort out the faces pretty quickly. Even if they don't always get the proper relationship, they inherently understand these people are somehow a part of their world.

Think about your own childhood. Do you remember your great-grandparents? Great-aunts and uncles? I remember large family gatherings with lots of relatives present. No doubt at that time I didn't fully understand how we were related, but I knew they were family. The memories of those gatherings are still with me today.

Smaller family gatherings allowed for greater understanding of the various relationships. Over time I was able to link the assorted branches of my extended family. As you can see, family reunions and dinners were a big part of my childhood. Planning reunions was important to my mother. And to her mother. Today, reunions are not as frequent as in the past, but we still get together as often as possible.

Children inherit the values of their parents. Family. Faith. Athletics. Music. Culture.

Children are copy cats. What they see from mommy and daddy often ends up within their own sets of likes and dislikes.

My parents loved to travel. I love to travel. My mother was an artist. She loved oil painting in particular. While I did not inherit her artistic talents, I did inherit her creative tendencies. She loved arts and crafts. As a young girl, I would help her make decorations for family gatherings and special occasions. I still love arts and crafts. She also loved genealogy. I followed her down that path, and added my own dimension to an avocation that is immensely satisfying.

To start our children down the path of interest in family history, it is important that we plan. Don't leave it to chance.

Openly engage in family history projects, talk

about ancestors, share photos and stories. Over time your child will most likely absorb that interest also, though it may not be apparent until they are older. Preschoolers love story time. School-age children often have homework assignments that can easily incorporate some bits of family history. It is not uncommon for teens to do interviews with a grandparent. These activities could be the beginning of a life-long love affair with family history.

Yes, we have all read the same thing in a magazine, newspaper article or online: "Children learn more quickly in their early years than at any other time in life." It's never too soon to start teaching our children about the value of family history.

2

Steady Tiny Steps Will Help Them Learn

Genealogy is a big word. A rather complex concept for children. Explaining it to a 3, 4 or 5-year-old will take some time. Remember how long it takes to teach them to count to 100? With a gentle yet persistent approach, children can understand the basics of genealogy that will grow right along with them. And hopefully, by the time the child is a pre-teen, he or she should have a fairly good grasp of the term and its significance.

Whatever age your child is, the following are a

few questions you will undoubtedly hear and need to answer.

"Mommy, what is genealogy?"

It's called a family tree for a reason. A full-grown tree is an instructive, tangible illustration of what genealogy is and makes a superb visual for children.

If weather permits, take your child outside. Lay in the grass under a mature tree with lots of branches. Just lay there for a bit and look at the tree. Then start to point out the trunk, the limbs, the smaller branches and then the smallest branches. If the child is asking questions about the tree, try to correlate those comments to the "family tree" you want the child to understand.

After a while begin to explain how your "family tree" is much like the real tree with lots of branches. Give the branches names that the child will recognize. After you have named one or two branches, see if the child can add some names. You might want to add that someday, when the child is older and has children of his or her own, they too will become branches in the family line.

Now, take your child into the house and draw your family tree on a large poster board. Keep it simple at first: the child's name, siblings, parent's names and grandparents' names. That's probably enough to begin with. Keep the poster board in a room where the child will see it often. Add more names (branches) as you think the child is ready. If, for example, a great-grandparent comes to visit, be sure to add that name as soon as possible so the child can link the visit with the individual(s). Add small photos when possible.

"Grandma, what is an ancestor?"

Ancestors are people we are related to, but most of them have died because they lived a long time ago; they are also called our forefathers. Ancestors were alive before we were born. Ancestors come before us in the family tree.

A trip to your family cemetery may not sound like a fun excursion for a little one. But it is possible to make it fun as well as educational. If it happens to be winter and there is snow on the ground, make snow angels and talk about the "family angels" as you walk through the headstones of your ancestors.

If it is a pretty summer day, take along a picnic lunch. As you walk through the cemetery, point out the names of those who are relatives, explaining that those people are ancestors. If possible, take a bouquet of flowers and have the child place individual flowers on the graves of their ancestors. No matter what the weather is like, impress on the child that cemeteries are places where we show respect for our ancestors.

If it is not possible to go to a cemetery, you might

take some photos of your family cemetery. Look at the pictures and talk about the names on the headstones. Find the ones that belong to your family and discuss how they are ancestors.

Now, go back to the poster board family tree. Add names and talk about where these people fit into the genealogy.

"Daddy, what is a descendant?"

A descendant is someone who is an offspring of a family member. Children are offspring. Children are descendants.

Do you have a family photo with three genera-tions? That would be a good place to start. Point to the grandparents then to their children. Then point to the parents and to their children. Again, bring out the poster board family tree and talk about ancestors and descendants throughout several generations.

Children learn by seeing.

Place the poster-board family tree, along with a few photos, in a prominent place so the child will see it often. This will help fix the images and information in the mind of the child. Keep the "tree" handy and refer to it frequently.

Children learn by doing.

Children love craft projects: cutting and pasting, coloring, painting. In subsequent chapters, there are many activity ideas you can choose from to help your child learn about your family.

Children learn by playing.

Play games with your children and grandchildren. It is a common lament today that children spend way too many hours in front of a TV, computer screen or tiny screen on their phone or tablet. Offer them a chance to play a card game or board game and do something that will allow for interaction with yourself and other adults. My family loves to play all kinds of games. Ideas for games that will help teach your children about family history can be found in following chapters.

Children learn by hearing.

Children are enthralled with stories, so watch for opportune moments that allow you to share a story.

I remember stories my Grandmother Korn told me about her childhood. She was raised in Fort Wayne, Indiana, and lived in a large two-story house. Directly behind the house was a cemetery. From her upstairs bedroom, she would often see lantern lights flickering in the evening darkness as grave robbers dug for gold and treasures among the dead. She remembered being frightened; I have remembered her stories for well over sixty years.

When I was a pre-teen I was totally intrigued by

the funny stories my dad and his brothers told while sitting around the kitchen table: antics of young boys growing up on the farm and the hilarious scrapes they got into as youngsters. I promised myself then that one day I would write a book about my dad's family. Even so, did I truly realize the stories were directly related to such a lofty topic as genealogy and family history? Was there a consciousness about my interest? Assuredly the answer is no. I just loved the stories! But, the seed was planted. Over time it bore fruit.

Make story telling an integral part of your family life. Stories can be humorous. They can be sad. They can have an important moral value or they can be downright silly. JUST TELL STORIES - whenever and as often as you can.

Instilling an interest in family history won't happen overnight, or even in a year or two. It will take a concerted effort over a lengthy period of time. And even then, there are no guarantees that when the child is an adult he or she will still be interested in family history.

But not making that effort seems like just hoping for the best down the road. Would we do that with our faith? Would we do that with math, English and science? Of course not! We send them to school. We take them to church or synagogue. We encourage them along the way. Why should our cherished family gene-alogy and stories be any different?

It's never too soon to start taking those steady steps to teach them the value of our family history.

3

Preschoolers and Kindergarteners

Kids love doing craft projects and playing games. Both can be used to teach them about family history. The remainder of this chapter describes some fun activities you can create to entertain and teach your young ones.

Match Game
Idea from Michelle Bryner, Las Vegas, Nevada.

Most kids have played this game in one form or another and it has several different names. The idea is to place "cards" face down then try to match them by turning over two cards at a time; if they don't match, then turn them face down again. The next player gets to turn over two cards and try to find two that match. The player who discovers the most matches wins the game.

Preparation by an adult:

You will need cardstock, regular white printer paper, scissors and glue. If you are making the cards by hand you will need all of the above plus a fine tip marker. The following instructions are for making the cards on the computer, but steps will be similar if you are making them by hand.

1. Open a new word document on your computer.
2. Click on page layout, portrait position, make the margins as small as possible.
3. Click on Insert.
4. Click on Table.
5. Choose the 3x3 table and click.

6. Click on border styles and choose the color of ink, then the specific border design you like best. You will then click the little pen icon onto each line of the table to get the color and design you have chosen.

7. Drag the table to the size you want, I made mine to fill an entire page. Three boxes across and three up and down. Try to make all as equal in size as possible.

8. Type into each box a name for the game. I typed: "The Niggemeyer Family Match Game." Put the title in a large bold print and center on each square.

9. Print on heavy cardstock, color of your choice.

10. Cut with paper cutter.

Select 10 or 12 photos (or more if you like) of multiple generations of your family. Scan the photos and place in a folder on your desktop. Print two of each photo in a size that will fit on the backs of the cards you have just made. Photos can be of people, homes, family artifacts, a significant vacation spot or any other place that has been especially important to your family. Kids love to see themselves in pictures, so make sure two or three of your photos include the children who will be playing the game. Print the names on the card with a fine tip marker; or, in a Word document place the photo and text together and print.

The Niggemeyer Family Match Game	The Niggemeyer Family Match Game	The Niggemeyer Family Match Game
The Niggemeyer Family Match Game	The Niggemeyer Family Match Game	The Niggemeyer Family Match Game
The Niggemeyer Family Match Game	The Niggemeyer Family Match Game	The Niggemeyer Family Match Game

Great grandma Mildred and Connor 2005	Great grandma Mildred and Connor 2005	Niggemeyer cousins Newark, Ohio 1973
Niggemeyer cousins Newark, Ohio 1973	Louis K. Niggemeyer Born Oct 3, 1897	Louis K. Niggemeyer Born Oct 3, 1897
Chuck Niggemeyer 2 years old.	Chuck Niggemeyer 2 years old.	Louis and Mildred Niggemeyer 1924

Preparation involving children:

Cut out the photos (and names, if they are added to the photos). Glue to the backs of the cards. Kids will be able to help with the gluing. Be sure to talk about the family photos as you cut and glue. Let dry. Then using lamination sheets, laminate the cards, cut and trim.

You probably won't even have to explain the rules. Just play the game and have fun!

Paper Chains – We Are All Linked Together!

Kids love making paper chains. I remember making them for holidays. And I remember my own children making paper chains to decorate the Christmas tree. Unfortunately, I didn't think back then about incorporating the project with a lesson in family history! And it is so simple.

Preparation by an adult:

Depending on how many chains you are making, and the length of the chains, you will need to buy one or two packages of construction paper. Color choices will be determined by the event you are preparing for. If you are putting up paper chains for a 4th of July party, you will probably want red, white and blue. Using a paper cutter, cut the construction paper into 1 ½ to 2 inch wide strips.

Print small photos (one inch) of members of your family onto regular white printer paper. You will need lots of photos, so place several on one page before printing.

Preparation involving children:

Have the child cut out each photo; again, talk about the family members as you are cutting. Paste one photo in the center of each strip. Paste the ends of the strip, link with the next one until the chain is the desired length.

When the chain is completed and put in place, have the child explain to someone else what it represents.

Are there any special ancestors or relatives they want to point out, and why?

Show and Tell

Ask your preschoolers or kindergarteners what their favorite part of school is and they will most likely say, "recess." Second most favorite? I suspect it could be "show and tell." Kids love taking something to school and sharing their special treasures with their teacher and friends.

So why not plan a show and tell of your own? Plan a "tea party" or an ice cream party and invite your little ones. They would undoubtedly be very impressed with special handmade invitations. Tell them to bring a favorite treasure to talk about and show everyone. Of course, your contribution to the show and tell will be a family keepsake, along with a photo of the owner if possible. It might be a piece of china, a painting done by someone in your family or even an old tool from great-grandpa's tool shed. Talk about the individual who owned the piece and describe how it was used. Why is it important to you? Make sure they understand how that person fits into your family tree.

Planning a party is always fun. Planning a party for young children/grandchildren is beneficial as well as fun. Use your imagination and come up with a fun-filled hour or two they will enjoy, learn from and hopefully remember forever.

Easter Egg Hunt

We are all familiar with this popular activity. It's fun for the kids, and fun for the adults who watch them bounce across a grassy lawn looking for brightly colored eggs to fill their baskets.

Traditionally, eggs are hard boiled and brightly decorated. Often plastic eggs are part of the hunt and are filled with small candies, or maybe money. Why not include in some of those plastic eggs a piece of family history or a photo?

Was someone in your family born on Easter Day? Or born in the same month as Easter? Was anyone in your family a pastor? Maybe there is a specific church that is associated with your family. Any of these could be incorporated into a short family history story. It doesn't have to be long. Just interesting. Photos, of course, help when you have them.

If you are having a summer family reunion, you might want to adapt the Easter egg hunt and do something similar as an activity for those rambunctious preschoolers. For any of our patriotic holidays you could make "firecrackers" from toilet paper tubes. Decorate and fill with candies and family history stories. Secure the ends with tape; add a construction paper cone on one end and red crepe paper streamers to the other. If you have lots of children and several stories, set aside time after all have been collected and read the stories together.

I suspect many of you can come up with your own ideas. Take advantage of unique family traditions that you can expand on and infuse with family history. Above all, have fun with whatever kinds of activities you come up with.

Make a Picture Book

Young children love to be read to. For years, I read to my own children at night before they went to sleep. I did the same thing with my grandchildren. It is comforting, great bonding time and teaches them the joy of reading. By making your own book for them, it can teach them some family history.

The picture book I made for my granddaughter is called: *The ABCs of My Family*. It contains photos of Jocelyn, her ancestors, family members and some family keepsakes. Everything in the book relates to her. Some of the photos are of ancestors going back several generations, many are of her and her family today.

Start this project by doing some preliminary work with a piece of paper, writing down every letter of the alphabet, then looking for photos and ideas. Some letters were obvious; others took some brainstorming.

I love looking through old family photos. I also proudly display many family heirlooms about the house. Correlating the photos or items I had chosen to highlight with the letters of the alphabet, and then adding appropriate text, was at times challenging. But it was also fun!

For me, the letters J and T were not readily apparent and were among the last of the letters that I was able to attach to a specific photo and memory. I slowly made my way from room to room in the house. As I looked over a variety of family keepsakes, two items suddenly jumped out at me: J, for the jug that my father used as a boy to fetch vinegar from the little village grocery store; and T, for the teddy bear that was my husband's as a child.

Once I had determined the photos and mementoes

to be used, I headed to the computer. I was ready to start my book.

First of all, scan all your photos if they are not digital copies already. Open a folder on your desktop and put all the photos into a folder that you want to use in your book.

I used Microsoft Publisher for my book, but it can be done in MS Word, MS PowerPoint or any other software package that combines text with graphics. Use the computer software that you are already familiar with.

Choose a cardstock for the front and back cover pages in the color of your choice. I used regular white printer paper for the inside pages.

As you begin working, allow yourself to get as creative with each page as you wish. My book was simple and straightforward. I placed one letter of the alphabet in an extra-large font, then added varying colors to the background of each letter. On a few of the pages I added some clip art that helped express the sentiment of that particular letter. Each page had at least one photo, identifying text and a bit of a story. You get to create your pages however you wish! Here's how to start.

1. Open a new document in the portrait position.

2. Change the margins of the document by going to custom margins. Set to:

   - Left, 1 inch

   - Right, 1 inch

   - Top, 0.2 inches

   - Bottom, 6 inches

     - These custom margins will place your pages in the top center which will allow you to print back to back once the book is completed.

3. Start with the cover page which can be a heavy card stock. I put the title of the book plus my

granddaughter's name on the front. Your computer will count this as page 1.

4. On page 2, I featured a photo of my granddaughter and myself. Be sure to include your name and the date when you made the book.

5. Page 3 on your computer will actually be the first page of the book. For the alphabet book, that would be the letter "A."

6. Arrange the photos and letters on each page as you desire. I switched the background colors, positions of the text and photos so that each page had a bit of variety.

7. You will have 28 pages total once you add all the letters of the alphabet.

8. Proof read every page to be sure you have names and dates correct.

9. Once you are satisfied with each page, you are ready to print. Print only two or four pages at

first to make sure they are printing properly. You want them back to back. Depending on your printer, you may have to insert them individually and by hand to have them printed correctly.

- Note: if you prefer, you can have the pages printed at a commercial printing establishment. You will need to convert your manuscript to a PDF and download to a thumb drive or disc. It could be expensive, so ask beforehand for an estimate of the cost.

10. After all pages are printed, trim them individually on a paper cutting board. I cut the bottom and right sides of each page making the finished book 5¼ x 8 inches.

11. Cut one piece of the card stock you used for the cover to those same dimensions and use for the back cover.

12. Take to an office supply store. I had the front

and back covers laminated (about $2) and had the book spiral bound ($5).

You can make your own book using the directions above, or by using any number of commercial photo book companies such as Blurb or Shutterfly which are easily found on the internet. Another choice might be My Publisher which provides a good template for both photos and text. Other options abound. Enter "photo books" into any search engine and it will give you a wide variety of alternatives to choose from.

I was quite happy with the end result of my home-made book. And best of all, my granddaughter loved it! Yours does not have to be an alphabet book. I suspect you may have lots of other ideas about family homes, pets or vacation spots that are dear to your family. Any of those ideas will work well to make a picture book for a preschooler.

The ABCs of my family.

Jocelyn

When my great-grandfather, Bill Korn, was a young boy, one of his

Jobs was to carry this **J**ug to the

little village grocery store for his mother and have it filled with vinegar.

Jigsaw Puzzles for Children of All Ages

Another favorite pastime for my family has been working on jigsaw puzzles together. Nearly all year long there is a puzzle on a table in our home. Working on puzzles provides time together without digital interference. Working on puzzles as a family encourages conversation and laughter, especially when I have been looking for a specific piece and my 15-year-old grandson comes into the room and finds it immediately!

Putting puzzles together is good for our minds. Adding some family history photos to the mix boosts the benefits.

Go to the internet, plug in the phrase "make jigsaw puzzle from photo." You will find an enormous number of resources for making personalized puzzles. You can make 12-piece puzzles for children, magnetic puzzles for children, chunky puzzles for children and older adults. You can find options for 12-piece to 1000-piece puzzles. You can make collages with several photos, or use one large photo that perhaps is your favorite. The collage puzzle will provide you the opportunity to place ancestors alongside the current generation.

The toughest part will most likely be choosing the photo or photos you want for your puzzle. Pets? Ancestral homes? A favorite vacation spot? A collage with ancestors? Or maybe a photo of a keepsake that represents a specific family story?

Pick a photo. Make a puzzle. Have some good-old-fashioned family fun.

4

Elementary School Students

Children are naturally curious. A word they all learn early in life is: "Why?" Followed closely by: "Grandpa, what is _____?" By the time they get to elementary school their curious natures are nourished by both parents and teachers.

Project based learning, as I discovered through my grandchildren, is a fairly new term, but the actual approach has been around for years. One could even argue, for centuries. Learning through doing. According to the Edutopia.com website: "In K-12 education, project-based learning has evolved as a method of instruction that addresses core content through rigorous, relevant, hands-on learning." Kids love it. And it works.

I suspect that you too can think of many ways to teach your children the joy and value of family history by engaging in physical projects or playing games. Below are a few of my own ideas to get you started.

School Geography Projects

A few years ago, my grandson came home from school and announced that he had a project for his fifth-grade geography class. He said, "I want to do Germany." Music to my ears since we have a lot of German heritage.

His assignment was to make a large poster board collage of things he researched about Germany. Of course, he included the usual things like finding a map, their national flag, what kinds of food they eat, manufacturing and agricultural facts, and customs of the country. I encouraged him to add a section about his family who emigrated from Germany to the United States in 1860. I had some photos for him to choose from, the name of the ship that carried them from Germany to the U. S. and where they eventually settled in Ohio. It was a tiny part of his overall project, but it did emphasize to him that his family had once lived there. Hooray! Family history!

Activity Placemats

If restaurants can do it, so can we. Certainly, you have been to any number of restaurants that offer paper placemats and crayons to the kids when they walk through the door. They know how antsy the kids can get while waiting for their meals. They also figured out that giving them some games and pictures to color keeps them quiet and engaged while they wait.

Dinner at home doesn't necessarily entail that kind of wait. But, we can take a cue from those restaurant activity placemats. Kids love them! Once again, adding family history serves a two-fold purpose.

Making placemats with some family history is an easy project which starts (as usual) with choosing a topic, choosing some photos and gathering information. I chose to make a placemat for my youngest grandchild, Cooper, and focused on my grandfather who was the founder of a family business that lasted nearly 100 years.

I also believed that the Korn Lumber Company was a good topic because my grandson has little knowledge of a working sawmill. His great-great grandfather, William F. Korn, was the founder, the head sawyer, the bookkeeper and knowledgeable lumberman. I didn't go into great detail about any of those elements, but did describe what a head sawyer is and some other interesting tidbits about the lumber business.

Along with the photos and information about the company and William F., I included a word game, some coloring pages and a brief genealogical line (with photos) so Cooper could readily identify how he is related.

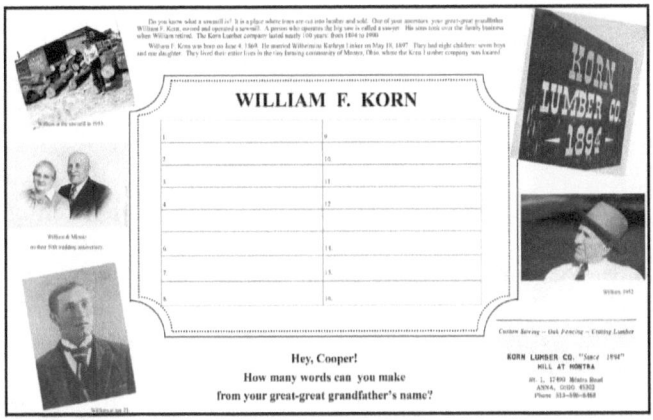

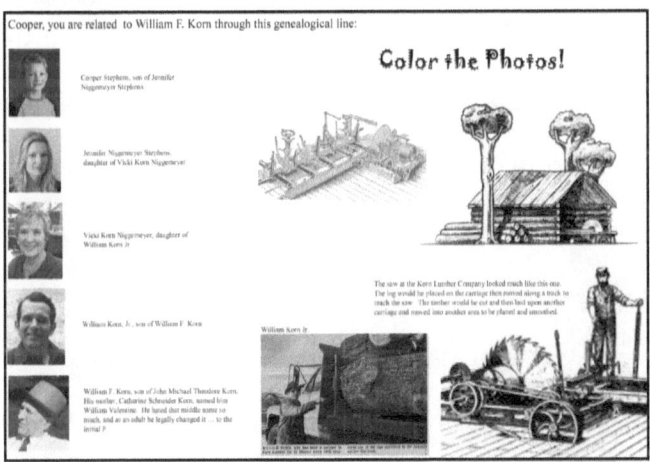

Once you have chosen your theme, photos and pertinent information, assemble your ideas by doodling on a scrap piece of paper to help visualize the completed project. I placed several photos at random, leaving space for identifying text along with historical facts.

Once you have an idea of placement, you can begin cutting and pasting, or inserting photos to your computer page. I chose to put the name game in the center of the placemat, but you certainly can place it anywhere. I found some coloring pages on the internet to include.

Open a document on your computer, it can be MS Word, MS Publisher or any program that will allow for both text and graphics. Place mats typically measure 14" x 18", so your first step will be to choose a larger page size. To make the name game, insert a table with two columns and as many rows as you desire. Drag the table to the size you prefer, making sure the boxes are as even as possible. (See additional directions below for the verbal word game.)

Be sure to have the completed placemat laminated, provide some dry erase markers, and suddenly it's a great gift!

Written Word Games

Veggies are good for kids, but they don't always like them. So, we disguise them as best we can. Kids don't typically like spelling tests either, but playing a game with words helps them learn while they are having fun. Adding some family history brings another dimension to this fun and beneficial game.

"How Many Words Can You Find From ____?" was a game I played as a child. I remember elementary teachers putting a word or two on the blackboard and we would be required to come up with as many words as we could by using just those letters. Looking back, it was probably just to take up some time so the teacher could concentrate on other things. But, I enjoyed it. It was fun, and no doubt helpful as well.

My idea for the word game on the activity placemats continued to develop, and eventually that thought turned into a word game booklet with several pages. I combined names of ancestors with names of places and events that are pertinent to our family stories.

Much like the Match Game (in chapter three), I started with a scrap piece of paper and began writing the names of people and places I wanted to include in the word game book. Then I searched for pictures. Scan all the photos you will need if they are not digitized already. Open a folder on your desktop and insert all the photos that you want to use in your book.

I designed a front cover for the word game booklet using a combination of graphic designs, the title of the game booklet and my grandson's name. The first page inside was devoted to Connor's genealogical line along with photos of him, his father, my husband and myself. I also emphasized that every page of the word puzzle book represented a person or place that was relative to his ancestral heritage. Be sure to place your own name and the date of the project somewhere on the page.

The next step was to make my template for the puzzle pages. I typically work with Publisher, but MSWord or any software that combines text and graphics will work.

1. Open a new document in the portrait position.

2. Change the margins of the document by going to custom margins. Set to:
   - Left, 0.5
   - Right, 0.5
   - Top, 0.8
   - Bottom, 0.4

3. Draw a text box at the top of the page. Make it about two inches from top to bottom and stretch it from one side to the other. This space will be for your family info and a small photo.

4. Draw another text box just below, about one inch from top to bottom, again stretching from one side to the other. This space is for the family

member's name for that particular puzzle page.

5. Click on Insert.

6. Click on Table.

7. Choose 4 columns x 15 rows.

8. Click on line color and choose the color of ink you want for your table lines.

9. Click on border. You want the "all lines" so that each space is outlined. You will then click the little pen icon onto each line of the table to get the color you have chosen for outlining each rectangle.

10. Drag the table to the size you want. I used the entire bottom of the page for the template as that is where the children will write in the words. Try to make all as equal in size as possible.

11. Once your template is made, copy and paste onto subsequent pages.

ELEMENTARY SCHOOL STUDENTS

Like the photo book above, a heavy card stock works well for both the front and back covers of the book. Print all pages on the inside on regular white printing paper. I designed my word game book to be spiral bound at the top, like a stenographer's notebook, and had both the front and back pages laminated (about $7 total.)

My grandsons have enjoyed the challenge of seeing how many words they can make from two or three words. If you too like word puzzles, you might want to make a copy for yourself!

Connor, you are related to every person mentioned in this word game book. Some through Papa Chuck, others through Grandma Vicki. The places mentioned are all relevant to your ancestral heritage.

John Connor Niggemeyer

John Christopher Niggemeyer,
father of John Connor.

Charles Milton Niggemeyer,
father of John Christopher.
Niggemeyers
Paderborn, Germany
Athens County, Ohio

Vicki Ann Korn Niggemeyer
mother of John Christopher.
Korns
Worthingtons
Andersons
Pence
The Old Brick

Louis Kenneth Niggemeyer (1897-1990) was born to John B. and Sara
Niggemeyer. Louis lived in Athens County, Ohio, until his retirement in 1962.
He and his wife Mildred Nuzum Niggemeyer then moved to Tarpon Springs,
Florida. Louis was a farmer most of his life, worked for a short period of time
at an explosives plant during WWII, then worked for Ohio Fuel and Gas
Company in 1946. Louis was your great-grandfather, Papa Chuck's father.

How many words can you make?

Louis Kenneth Niggemeyer

Verbal Word Games

If you travel a lot, like my family did, and you find yourself in the car with your kids, it is the perfect time to play some verbal games. Years ago, we didn't have iPhones, electronic tablets or built-in screens to watch movies while we traveled. We were a captive audience to the adults in the front of the vehicle. We played word games.

One of my favorites was: "My father owns a grocery store, and in it he sells _____." My kids loved that game too. Each person announces an item, the next person repeats that item and adds one more. The next person repeats both of those and adds another. It's a fun game as well as a game that makes the brain work. How about playing that same game using family names and places? For example: "My grandmother owns a photo album and in it she has pictures of _____."

Trivia games are easily tweaked to family history and can be played anywhere without any prompts.

Just questions and answers. Who can come up with a family name, and who can guess it? Let's call it: "I am thinking of _____."

Let your imagination soar! I am sure you will come up with plenty of ideas for games that can be tweaked to incorporate family.

Make Your Own Board Games

If your family loves to play board games, think about making a game using your specific family history. You can make it yourself, or have one custom designed for you.

Children often make games with construction paper, cardboard, markers and some glue. If you want to make an interesting board game for your children, tap into that same childlike imaginative process.

How about a Familopoly game with squares representing various branches of your family names, family businesses or favorite vacation spots? How about a board treasure hunt game that follows a path? First person to get to the treasure wins. If the player answers questions correctly, he/she moves forward; if not, he/she remains on the same spot. The fun of making up a game is that you can make up your own rules!

Bingo is another game you can incorporate by making cards on large pieces of card stock. You can use a ruler and draw your game boards, or make them on the computer by using a table format, print and glue onto the card stock. Make the squares with family names, favorite vacation spots, names of pets or any significant family element.

To assemble any of these games, identify some family facts and print them onto cardstock then cut to the size you need. Laminating them would help preserve their lifespan. If you need money, make your own, or purchase packages of pre-printed play money at most discount stores.

For the game board itself, choose a thin piece of wood paneling. Sand any rough, jagged edges. You could also use a heavy-duty poster board. Another option is to buy a game at a discount or thrift store and just use the board. Replace the graphics on the board with family photos or pertinent facts. Once all your game components are printed and ready, glue to the surface of your game board. Place a decoupage coating to protect it.

Most games need tokens/characters to move along the game board. Let your kids help make these by using empty thread spools, plastic bottle caps or buy an inexpensive set of erasers with an assortment of figures. If you are making your own, provide the kids with a wide assortment of crafty items you have on hand: yarn, tiny buttons, sequins, paint and lots of glue! If you are gluing onto plastic, you might need to use hot glue. Young children would need some assistance from an adult.

Children love making up games. But if it sounds too daunting to you, your other option is to have a personalized game made for you, using your ideas and information. There are several websites that offer personalized games. Plug into your search engine the words: "make your own board game." Lots of ideas with a wide variety of pricing will keep you busy as you search for the perfect match to your concept.

Think of any game that your family enjoys, then tweak it to incorporate family history. Let your kids help. Make it a collaborative effort, which by itself will make for some fun family time. Roll the dice and let the games begin!

Set Up a Treasure Hunt

Treasure hunts have been a popular diversion for kids for many years. But it does take some careful thought and planning; especially since the primary goal is to incorporate some family history into this activity.

Once again, start with a pad of paper. I slowly walked throughout our house and yard area. Ours is small, you might have a much larger piece of property with many more options than I had. Still, I found some great places to "hide" the clues. I noted nine places for hiding the clues, plus the treasure spot.

I chose family pieces that were not fragile as places for hiding the clues: a wooden goat, a piece of furniture that belonged to my grandmother, a couple of pictures, a bird house made from the siding of an old family home, a piece of horse harness that hangs on the wall. You get the idea.

The next step was to create the clues. That took me a while. You want the clues to be spread all over the area to make the kids go from one room to another, outside if possible, back and forth. So, I numbered my clues to correspond with the concept of going from one side of the house to the other. I also took the extra time to write my clues in little jingles. I am not a poet, but I do love to write short verses and jingles when I have an opportunity.

Once the clue has been solved, and the children have found the first item, the card they find will describe the family piece, followed by the next clue. Here is an example.

KIDS AND FAMILY HISTORY

Clue #1:

Come look at us!

It's easy to see that our family was quite big.

Tall ones, thin ones, small ones too,

ladies and gents were we.

We lined up nicely in front of our home,

wearing our very best,

Come look at us!

A beautiful family for all the world to see.

Once the item has been found, the history of the item will be on top of the page with another clue below it.

History of clue #1: This photo of the John B. Niggemeyer family was taken sometime around 1902 in front of their home in Athens County, Ohio. This was the first John B. who would have been your great-great-great grandfather.

Clue #2: _and so on._

After all the clues were typed, I printed them off and folded them, ready to insert in the appropriate places.

I found a terrific spot for the "treasure" and placed some candy and enough gift cards for all the grandkids once they had found it. Of course, the "treasure" can be anything you choose. Depending on the ages of the children, the treasure can be small trinkets found in the dollar bins at your local discount store, candy, interesting pencils and erasers, money or gift cards.

Make Your Own Sports Playing Cards

Collecting sports players' cards has been a popular hobby for young boys (and some not so young!) for several decades. Do you have someone in your family who played sports? Someone who played in high school or college, but never made it to the pros? Here is your opportunity to put those ancestors in the spotlight by creating trading cards for them. You can make your own on your computer using a photo along with facts about the individual, or let the professionals do it by going to any number of sites on the internet. Bighugelabs.com specializes in ideas of things to do with photos, including making sports cards. You can also look at Make Your Own Sports Cards or Personalized Sports Photos Trading Cards.

If your family is a sports loving group, this project should be well received.

Intertwine Family History with Poetry

A couple of years ago my husband and I were traveling through Ohio. While driving through the countryside I kept seeing abandoned houses. It reminded me of a poem that I learned when I was in fifth grade: "The House With Nobody In It" by Joyce Kilmer.

I began taking pictures of the sad-looking,

run-down abandoned houses. I also took several photos of my husband's original family home and farm buildings. When we got home I put the photos together with the poem and made a book for the kids and grandkids. It encompassed some of my history from my elementary years, some of my husband's family history and the poem that I had long loved.

I chose to have this book made commercially through My Publisher, and ordered 10 of them. It is a small book, only 20 pages in full color and glossy finish. It was a perfect gift!

Do you have ancestors who were blacksmiths? Teachers? Sailors? Preachers? Soldiers? There's a wealth of old poetry that captures the essence of those professions in years gone by. For example: "The Village Blacksmith" by Henry Wadsworth Longfellow.

You may have to do some research to find the exact poem you want, but as we all know by now, search engines are marvelous tools for those of us who are researching specific topics.

Fortunately for me, Joyce Kilmer's poem is no longer under copyright rules. It is part of what is called public domain. According to copylaw.com, any written works that were published prior to 1923 are now considered public domain and can be used freely.

If you are making just a few books for family only, you may not need to worry about a copyright on the poem you choose. However, I encourage you to check out two sources that can help you make that determination. Go to copylaw.com and/or to the U.S. Copyright Office site (www.copyright.gov/fls/fl102.html) to read what is called the Fair Use Doctrine. Both sites will help you determine what you are legally allowed to use in your work.

5

Teens

It often seems that teens, and even preteens, speak a different language than the rest of us. At times, it seems they often don't want to be seen with anyone over age 20! Let alone talk to us! Still, they are "our" teens and we need to try our best to spend time with them and have meaningful conversations.

Of all the things I am learning from my teenage grandchildren, I have definitely discovered that if I want to engage with them I must learn their language. I now have a smart phone, I have learned to text and send photos, and I am learning the ropes of social media.

Teens simply have no desire to open a family history book and read. But - they are receptive to bits and pieces of information that can be disseminated through Facebook, Instagram or other social media outlets.

If you are not yet savvy about social media, here is a wonderful opportunity for a conversation with your teens that they will welcome. Ask for suggestions about the kinds of social media they use. Do they have suggestions for you? Ask for their help in setting up the apps. As adults, we tend to think we teach them. And we do! But clearly in this case, they can teach us so much about the new technological world we all live in.

So, my advice to you - try learning their language!

Social Media

While those of us in the older generation recognize both the pros and cons of social media, most teens find social media irresistible for engaging and keeping up with their friends. Girls especially seem devoted to their phones, swapping photos and youthful chatter. I maintain that this pervasive social "force" can also be employed for spreading family history.

While visiting with my granddaughter recently, the two of us talked about social media and how it could be utilized for conveying small pieces of family history. Would she be interested in helping me with this little project? She immediately suggested we try Instagram.

Instagram is an online service that allows users to share photos, videos and limited comments on their smart phones. There's definitely not enough space to write a book! But it does allow for captions and small bits of critical information.

You can choose to make your Instagram account public or private. We have chosen to make ours private for obvious reasons, so that only invited family and friends can see our posts. I send my granddaughter the information and she does the rest! She's helping me. She's learning as she posts. And she's providing a service to other family members. All while doing something she loves to do.

Veteran's Day is a great example of the kinds of posts we put out there for family members. I sent her a photo of my father (her great-grandfather) who served during WWII. I sent the vital information about the years he served and where he served. As the "keeper" of the site it is her responsibility to use my information and post to the site.

Instagram is not the only option. Depending on the interests of your individual teen there are plenty of other social media outlets they might be knowledge-able about and more willing to use. Twitter, Tumblr and Flickr are similar to Instagram.

What is your teen interested in? What is his or her

specialty? Encourage them to help communicate family history by using any of these alternatives. But, beware of Snapchat, it self-destructs after opening! That would certainly be counterproductive for our goals.

Facebook is probably the most well-known of the social media sites. Adults and teens both can be found posting photos and updating friends about their lives. If you don't want everyone seeing your family posts, it is possible to open a page that is private. For additional information, go to your browser and insert: Can I Open a Family Account on Facebook? The site provides step-by-step instructions on how to set up a family account. If you have a teen who predominantly uses Facebook, ask if he/she would be willing to set up a family account. The benefit of a Facebook account is that everyone can contribute. You will be able to post also, but our objective here is to get teens involved. So, make a point to follow up with your teen, provide him or her with some family history and ask them to post it. The more they see and hear, the more they remember.

Clearly, daily posting on any kind of social media site is not mandatory. Frequency of posts is completely up to you. My granddaughter and I don't post on Instagram every day. Only occasionally. What is equally clear is that social media in any form is one more viable avenue for passing along family history; a form that has a good chance of getting our teens enthused and informed.

Design a Family Website

The very best thing about a family website is that it can be a one-stop information site for your family. A website is easy to use once it has been established. It can contain photos as well as large bodies of text. It can be easily updated with current dates for family activities and gatherings. A website is also a great place for blogging; a spot on the website where you can relate those ancestral stories as well as provide current news about your family.

Most young people are quite proficient at using the computer. Hopefully one of your kids or grand-kids would be willing, possibly even eager, to design a unique family website for you.

There are so many options for you to consider when setting up a family website that I believe my very best advice is to steer you to the internet. You will find dozens of sites for you to read through and consider. You and your teen should look over these sites before starting the process. Here are a few suggestions to get you started: thesitewizard.com; WebsiteBuildersTop10. com; or merely go to your browser and plug in the words: how to set up a personal webpage.

It will most likely seem daunting at first, but there are definite steps to the process. So, take it one step at a time! Give yourself time to absorb and learn.

You will need to start with a domain name and a web server, and there are many options for you to consider. There is a charge for securing a domain name, usually costing from $5 to $10 per year. There are free website servers; however, they will run advertisements on your site. Most website servers charge an annual fee. As you do your homework, make notes about the pros and cons of each. Your teen may already have some experience and can help decide which options are the best fit.

Design your website to suit your needs. Within your website you can create several easily accessible, individual pages. You can create a home page where you most likely will want to identify yourself and your teen along with the family name and branches you are reaching out to. You might want to convey why you think the website is important, and how it can be a good communication tool for your family. Some sites allow for comments from anyone accessing the page which makes for a nice running commentary among family members. You can add a news and events page, a type of bulletin board that family members will automatically go to for family news and activities. Design one page for blogging, this is where you can add stories of the past and the present. Definitely design a genealogy page for your family members to refer to. You can also insert a contact page with an email address so that your readers can easily contact you.

Once your website is up and running you can list family gatherings, weddings, births, deaths, photos, videos, genealogy, and most importantly, stories and ancestral history! You provide the information; your teen will learn by posting those precious family stories for everyone to enjoy.

Homework Interviews

A year ago my granddaughter called and asked if I would be willing to let her interview me. Her assignment was to talk to someone who remembered what it was like being in the eighth grade. Of course, I agreed. And then wondered if I truly could recall much of what I experienced as an eighth grader! I needn't have worried. Many fun, as well as painful, memories came back as I thought about it.

We set a time for the official interview. In the meantime, she had a list of questions that I could study and make some notes. It was very interesting for both of us. I learned a little about the teen scene of today while she was stunned by the teen scenes of my youth. Talk about a generation gap!

I often hear people talk about teens doing interviews of their parents and/or grandparents. What was life like? What did you do in Vietnam? What did you do in the Gulf War? What do you remember about Nixon resigning his presidency? Where were you on 9/11?

As the family historian, I was delighted to share my stories with my granddaughter. As a historian in general, I am highly gratified that teachers encourage our teens to interview and write these stories about their family members, even friends or neighbors.

When your teenage child or grandchild gets one of these assignments, take advantage of the situation and be a family-story cheerleader! Encourage good interview techniques. Make suggestions for saving the stories they write for future generations. Provide ideas for putting the story in print and saving it digitally as well. An interview can be turned into a booklet and given as a gift. Above all, let them know how pleased you are that they are undertaking the assignment.

Underscore how the assignment is more than just school work. Let them know this is a big part of being a family historian, and that their efforts will be greatly appreciated by yourself and future descendants.

Then, if they are receptive, provide some tools for the assignment.

A good interview starts with a specific set of questions. Avoid asking yes or no questions. The idea is to get the individual talking about his/her experiences, to provide a first-hand account of the experiences and the emotions generated. If possible, give a copy of the questions to the person being interviewed beforehand.

The interview with my granddaughter already had parameters set: what do you remember about being an eighth grader. If the student's teacher has not already assigned a specific focus, encourage your teen to come up with a clearly defined topic. The topic could be a specific experience, personal recollections of a major catastrophe he or she survived, an interesting profession, or places he or she has lived and/or traveled to.

On the other hand, if it is a generalized interview, the conversation can wander to many parts of the individual's life. And that's okay too. Make it a mini-biography. Where was he/she born? Where did the individual live? What kind of changes in the world has he/she seen? How did the person feel about those changes? Recall a favorite memory from childhood. From adulthood. Again, ask questions that illicit lengthy responses instead of a simple yes or no.

If possible, record the interview. Inexpensive digital recorders can be found online or at nearly any discount store in the electronics department. Recorders are handy devices for anyone who is interested in keeping family history. After the interview, the teen can either transcribe the tape or merely listen and make notes for the writing assignment.

Here is the most important part – save everything! Save the recording. Save the notes. Put the writing assignment in a binder or folder for future generations. Digitize and put on a disc or store in a cloud.

In addition to a clear title of the person who was interviewed, make sure the teen's name is on the paper along with the date of the interview.

This is not just a writing assignment. This is family history! And everyone - I repeat - *everyone* has interesting stories! Help your teen discover them. Make sure they are preserved.

Make a Video

Producing a video is an ideal way to save and share family history. Videos capture both sound and real-time images. A straightforward, no frills video will capture the conversation between the interviewer and the interviewee, and is a wonderful addition to the family archives. Just download to your PC, laptop or a thumb drive, watch and enjoy!

With a bit more time and effort, you and your teen can produce a mini-documentary. Along with the video, you can add old photos, maps and documents.

You can narrate the video and add background music. Whether the simple variety, or the enhanced version, the video can be preserved on a disc, thumb drive or in the cloud.

Making a video will require some forethought and planning. It is well worth the effort though for the teen who might be interested in learning about videography, photography or even technical skills, and is especially helpful for preserving family history.

In many ways, planning for a video is much like doing the homework interview as related above. Work with your teen to establish the objectives of the video. What is the topic? Who is the subject? Are you making a video based on one individual's life or an entire family?

Start with an outline of your idea. Where do you want to start? Where do you go next? How do you want to end the video? Do you have still shots from earlier years? Do you have maps or documents you want to include in the video? Write down step-by-step how you visualize the video from beginning to end.

Once you have the visual of where you want to go with the video, then turn your thoughts to the equipment. What do you already have? Do you have a good video camera? Smart phones definitely are capable of capturing short bursts of video, but if you want a truly good quality video, you should think about investing in a better device.

The prices of camcorders listed on the internet are unbelievably disparate, from under $100 to thousands of dollars. Some weigh as little as four ounces, others weigh up to one pound. Please think about this: if you don't have a good tripod, you could be holding the camera for lengthy periods of time.

All new model camcorders are digital, and the content can be easily downloaded onto your PC or laptop.

But there are differences. Do you want a camera with a hard drive that can hold multiple videos? Or do you prefer a camcorder with a flash drive or memory card that will hold a smaller amount of footage until you download onto your computer? Flash memory is solid state which makes it more durable; the hard disc version has moving parts which can be damaged if you drop the camera (http://www.desktop-documentaries.com/flash-memory-camcorders.html). Flash drives do not hold as much footage as a hard drive, and if you want to store footage on the cards, the memory cards are relatively expensive. Either way, you will most likely want to download your video onto your PC, laptop or tablet to make your video.

Again, I must steer you to the internet to research which camcorder will serve your needs the best. There are so many sites with good information that I hesitate to recommend one over the other. ConsumerReports.org might be a good place to start.

As you are combing through all this information, you will want to consider your budget, the size of the project and future use. How many videos do you think you and your teen will be making? Is this something you might want to pursue yourself as you compile your family history? No one can answer these questions but you.

Once you have your outline and have gathered your equipment, you are ready to put together a video. Explain to the individual or family what you are doing and the expectations. You might want to provide a copy of your outline so he or she will feel comfortable with the project. Ask if there are any questions. You don't want any surprises and unexpectedly find your subject refusing to go on with the video.

When all the footage is gathered, download onto your PC or laptop. Digitize all still shots, maps and documents that you wish to insert into the video. I used Windows Movie Maker for my own video, and all the still shots had to be JPEGs for insertion into the movie.

Windows Movie Maker is easy to use. It just takes some practice. If you have never made a movie, I suggest you play around with the software to see how it works; then make a short sample video. When you feel comfortable, you and your teen can start the project. Once the video is completed to your satisfaction follow the "prompts" to "make the movie," then burn to a disc or thumb drive.

If you have never done this kind of work, start small. As you gain confidence you can work your way up to bigger projects. Encourage your teen to be honest about his or her interest in the project. Is it something they will want to pursue beyond one interview? Many high schools today offer computer and videography courses. If they are taking those kinds of classes, they may be required to make several videos as class assignments.

In my book *Get Creative with Your Family History*, I devoted an entire chapter to digital documentation. It provides far more detail to the process of organizing and making a video than I have included here. I have made three digital photo albums/videos/documentary examples that can be viewed on my website: getcreativewithyourfamilyhistory.com. Check them out to see what you too can accomplish.

Making a video is undoubtedly one of the more time consuming and technically challenging undertakings that I am suggesting for you and your teen. But if you have a teen who is already interested, it can be a wonderful experience for everyone. Videos capture the living voices and images which a book just cannot convey. It's well worth the effort!

Journaling

Encourage your kids to journal. While I realize that isn't directly related to their ancestral history, they will be starting their own historical record. Anything that happens today is tomorrow's history!

When we are young, we think we will always remember the night we went on our first date. Our first prom. The vacation we took to Hawaii. However, as adults, we know that is just not the case. Certainly not the details anyway. Trip and personal journals are the answer.

I have purchased several journals for my grandkids over the years. Do they use them? I suspect not much. But, I still try.

When the kids were really young, I made trip journals for them before they left on a six-week journey through the western states' National Parks. You can buy composition tablets that have space at the top for drawings. I thought the kids would enjoy being able to draw something they had seen during the day, and then write a sentence or two. I personalized each journal with colorful wall paper samples, and was so excited about giving them to the grandkids! Again, I am not sure they used them. But I thought at the time it was a very nice idea.

As the grandkids have gotten older, they have gotten busier. As is true of all teens! They are active in school and sport activities. Some day they will look back on these exciting years and start wondering about the details. If they have kept a journal, the answers to those nagging questions can be found. If not, they'll most likely be gone forever.

That's why journals are so important. I am a sporadic journaler. So was my father. Even so, as I have worked on my family history projects, those journals of my dad's and grandfather's have been invaluable for finding specific dates and details of events in our lives. I am so grateful for the journals I do have, and wish fervently I had done more.

The journals that our children and grandchildren keep are their stories. Their stories are part of the family history. I don't nag, but I am still encouraging them to journal. That's all we can do. So, keep on tryin'!

6

Be Persistent, but Not Pushy

Intense interest in family history typically comes along later in life. As we get older we think more about our parents, our grandparents, our ancestry. The stories become more important to us. As we age, we start to recognize our own mortality, and with that comes the desire to preserve our own stories.

We must keep that in mind as we approach ways to get our children and grandchildren interested in family history. They most likely will not be as passionate about genealogy and family history as we are, but that does not mean we should not try to demonstrate its importance.

The activities and craft ideas in the previous chapters of this book are suggestions. They are not one-size-fits all. Some will be more suitable for your specific situations and challenges; others simply may not work at all. So, use what you can. Adapt and change what you need for your family.

How large is your family? Is a website practical if you have a small family? Is your family in one location or separated by many miles? How would that affect your choices? Does the activity you want to engage in fit your budget? What are the ages of your children and/or grandchildren? There are many factors at play. So, think about how these suggestions can be used to engage your own family. Determine which ideas will serve you best.

Above all – don't ever quit trying to convey the importance of family history.

Be persistent, but not pushy.

I first became interested in family history when I was 12 years old. I have vivid memories of sitting around the kitchen table with my dad and his brothers, listening to them tell tales of their childhood. I was mesmerized. My mother was a genealogist long before the internet made it much easier. We received letters from distant family members sharing births, deaths, dates and any scraps of stories they might have remembered. I remember making an audio recording of a distant cousin relating her brothers' adventures as early aviation pioneers.

I was not pushed into a fascination with family history. I was routinely exposed to it. And for me, it took! It has been my passion for the past 25 years.

Demonstrate, but don't demand.

Showing our children and grandchildren the joys of family history is one of the greatest gifts we can give them.

Demanding their interest will only turn them away. So, talk about the family stories, show them related items, but if they don't appear receptive - give them space. Maybe the moment isn't right. Try again another day.

Engage, but don't embarrass.

Children, like adults, are unique individuals. I know I get overly excited at times about a genealogical discovery or putting together pieces of information that reveal another family story. I want to shout it out to everyone I know! But not everyone gets as excited as I do.

As you engage in some of the projects I have suggested in this book, some kids will be super excited while others will not. Chiding those who are not showing the interest you had hoped for will be counterproductive. Don't embarrass one child by comparing them to another. Praise them all for the good work they have done.

Hopefully you now have a plan. Even so, the best of plans or the best of intentions don't always succeed. Unfortunately, we may never know if our attempts at introducing our children or grandchildren to family history will bear fruit. My parents knew. I had finished two family history books before they died, but that doesn't always happen.

You may never know which of your children or grandchildren will "pick up the pen" and carry on your work. I may never know. But, I choose to believe that someone will see the value and continue to capture our family stories. I choose to believe that someday they will be grateful that I kept the stories alive through books, videos and photo albums containing their heritage. I choose to believe that one day they will say, "thank you Grandma," even though I probably won't be around to hear them.

Acknowledgements

When I finished my last book, *Get Creative with Your Family History*, I did not have any plans for writing another book about family history projects. Yet, here I am.

Over the two years since *Get Creative* was first published, I have spoken to many groups about the value of getting our stories in writing and preserving them for future generations. I had also inserted into my program some things that might get our children engaged in this significant pastime. When I mentioned ideas for our children, many people in the groups responded favorably. I realized I had hit on something that resonated with parents and grandparents.

This book, *Kids and Family History*, is a result of that feedback. So, thank you to all of you who inspired me with your comments!

As usual, I have been blessed with many people who have encouraged and helped me with this book. I am extremely grateful to all of them.

Sue Hoge, my friend and DAR sister (Daughters of the American Revolution), has been very supportive of this work. Sue is an elementary school teacher by profession. She holds a Master's Degree in Education and has accumulated several years of experience in the classroom. She is also an author herself, *Play on Purpose*, a book about the value of playing and learning.

Dadee Burdick, my friend and neighbor who is very tech savvy has helped copy edit, proof and made sure my tech-ducks were all in a row! I couldn't have done this without her.

Dale Whalen, another friend and neighbor, is also a tech savvy individual I can count on to help me with questions. Dale is my webmaster, and gave me great advice in the section of this book about designing websites.

Betty Westby, my fellow-family-history-fanatic and dear friend of many years, always gives me solid constructive criticism, copy edits and proofs my manuscripts.

Jocelyn Stephens, my granddaughter, has been immensely helpful in teaching me how to use my iPhone and show me the positive aspects of social media. She is a dream granddaughter and I am forever grateful for her help and her love.

So many people have been supportive of this endeavor, but none more so than my husband, Chuck.

He calms me when I am in total frustration over the computer, and then patiently helps me figure out where I went wrong. He listens to me when I need to bounce ideas off someone else, and never complains when I do so. He reads my manuscripts and offers advice even though he's a science guy and a pilot, not a writer. He goes with me to my presentations, he carries equipment, helps me set up tables and serves as my cashier. He is there for me whenever I need him!

Thank you everyone who has had any part in this effort. I am grateful to have so many kind friends and such a loving family.